BOOKS BY ROBERT PENN WARREN

John Brown: The Making of a Martyr
Thirty-six Poems
Night Rider
Eleven Poems on the Same Theme
At Heaven's Gate
Selected Poems, 1923–1943
All the King's Men
Blackberry Winter
The Circus in the Attic
World Enough and Time
Brother to Dragons
Band of Angels
Segregation: The Inner Conflict in the South
Promises: Poems 1954–1956
Selected Essays
The Cave
All the King's Men (play)
You, Emperors, and Others: Poems 1957–1960
The Legacy of the Civil War
Wilderness
Flood
Who Speaks for the Negro?
Selected Poems: New and Old, 1923–1966
Incarnations: Poems 1966–1968
Audubon: A Vision
Homage to Theodore Dreiser
Meet Me in the Green Glen
Or Else—Poem/Poems 1968–1974
Democracy and Poetry
Selected Poems: 1923–1975
A Place to Come To
Now and Then: Poems 1976–1978
Brother to Dragons: A New Version
Being Here: Poetry 1977–1980
Jefferson Davis Gets His Citizenship Back
Rumor Verified: Poems 1979–1980

RUMOR VERIFIED

Poems 1979–1980

ROBERT PENN WARREN

RUMOR VERIFIED
Poems 1979–1980

RANDOM HOUSE NEW YORK

"Looking Northward, Aegeanward: Nestlings on Seacliff," "Paradox of Time: Gravity of Stone and Ecstasy of Wind; Law of Attrition; One I Knew," "Sunset Scrupulously Observed," "What Voice at Moth-Hour," and "Summer Afternoon and Hypnosis" originally appeared in *The New Yorker*.

"Rumor Verified" and "Summer Rain in Mountains" first appeared in *Antaeus*.

Other selections appeared in the following: *The American Poetry Review, The Atlantic Monthly, Conjunctions, The Georgia Review, Kentucky Poetry Review, Salmagundi, Sewanee Review, The Southern Review,* University of Kentucky Libraries (King Library Press), *Vanderbilt Poetry Review, Washington Post (Book World),* and *The Yale Review.*

Library of Congress Cataloging in Publication Data

Warren, Robert Penn, 1905–
  Rumor verified

  I. Title.
PS3545.A748R8   1981   811'.52   81–40216
ISBN 0–394–52136–6   AACR2
ISBN 0–394–74960–X (pbk.)
ISBN 0–394–52137–4 (limited)

Manufactured in the United States of America

2 3 4 5 6 7 8 9

First Edition

TO
PETER AND EBE BLUME

. . . io vidi delle cose belle
Che porta il ciel, per un pertugio tondo,
E quindi uscimmo a riveder le stelle,

Dante: *Inferno,* canto xxxiv

CONTENTS

I. PROLOGUE

　MEDITERRANEAN BASIN
　　1. Chthonian Revelation: A Myth　3
　　2. Looking Northward, Aegeanward: Nestlings on Seacliff　6

II. PARADOX OF TIME

　BLESSÈD ACCIDENT　11
　PARADOX OF TIME
　　1. Gravity of Stone and Ecstasy of Wind　13
　　2. Law of Attrition　14
　　3. One I Knew　16
　SMALL ETERNITY　19
　BASIC SYLLOGISM　20
　SITTING ON FARM LAWN
　　ON SUNDAY AFTERNOON　21

III. EVENTS

　GOING WEST　25
　NAMELESS THING　27
　RUMOR VERIFIED　29
　SUNSET SCRUPULOUSLY OBSERVED　31
　MINNEAPOLIS STORY　33
　MOUNTAIN MYSTERY　35
　CONVERGENCES　37

IV. A POINT NORTH

VERMONT THAW 43

CYCLE 45

SUMMER RAIN IN MOUNTAINS 47

VERMONT BALLAD: CHANGE OF SEASON 49

V. IF THIS IS THE WAY IT IS

QUESTIONS YOU MUST LEARN TO LIVE PAST 53

AFTER RESTLESS NIGHT 55

WHAT WAS THE THOUGHT? 57

DEAD HORSE IN FIELD 59

IMMANENCE 61

CORNER OF THE EYE 63

IF 65

VI. BUT ALSO

WHAT VOICE AT MOTH-HOUR 69

ANOTHER DIMENSION 70

GLIMPSES OF SEASONS

   1. Gasp-Glory of Gold Light 72

   2. Snow Out of Season 73

   3. Redwing Blackbirds 75

   4. Crocus Dawn 77

ENGLISH COCKER: OLD AND BLIND 78

DAWN 79

MILLPOND LOST 81

SUMMER AFTERNOON AND HYPNOSIS 83

VII. FEAR AND TREMBLING

IF EVER 87

HAVE YOU EVER EATEN STARS? 88

TWICE BORN 90

THE SEA HATES THE LAND 92

AFTERWARD 93

VIII. CODA

FEAR AND TREMBLING 97

I

PROLOGUE

* This symbol is used to indicate a space between sections of a poem wherever such spaces are lost in pagination.

MEDITERRANEAN BASIN

I. CHTHONIAN REVELATION: A MYTH

Long before sun had toward the mountain dipped,
There downward at crag-fall, bare-footed, bare-hided but for
Beach-decency's minimum, they
Painfully picked past lava, past pumice, past boulders
High-hung and precarious over the sea-edge, awaiting
Last gust or earth-tremor. Below,
Lay the sand-patch, white
As the lace-fringe that, languid and lazy,
Teased from the edge of the sun-singing sea.

Few know what is there:
Sea and sand finger back into cave-shade where
Gothic, great strata,
Once torn in the shudder of earth and earth-agony, had
Down-reached to find footing in depth. Now deep
In arched dusk from the secret strand, the eye
Stares from that mystic and chthonian privacy
To far waters whose tirelessly eye-slashing blue
Commands the wide world beyond that secret purlieu.

After sun, how dark! Or after sun-scimitar, how
Gentle the touch of the shade's hypothetical hand. Farther on,
Farther in!—and on the soft sand he is sure
Of the track. Then looks back
Just once through the dwindling aperture
To the world of light-tangled detail

3

Where once life was led that now seems illusion of life
And swings in the distance with no more identity than
A dream half-remembered. He turns. His face lifts
To the soaring and scarcely definable nave,
From which darkness downward and endlessly sifts.

Eyes lower: and there,
In that drizzle of earth's inner darkness, she
Stands, face upward, arms up as in prayer or
Communion with whispers that wordlessly breathe—
There in columnar gracility stands, breasts,
In that posture, high. Eyes closed. And in
Such world of shadows, she,
From the light of her own inner being, glows.

Slowly, the lifted arms descend, fingers out,
Slightly parted. His eyes find the light of her eyes,
And over immeasurable distance,
Hands out, as though feeling his way in the act,
On the soundless sand he moves in his naked trance.
At last, fingertips make contact.

When in hermetic wisdom they wake, the cave-mouth is dim.
Once out, they find sun sinking under the mountain-rim,
And a last gleam boldly probes
High eastward the lone upper cloud. Scraps of nylon
Slip on like new skin, though cold, and feet
Find the rustle and kitten-tongue kiss of the foam creeping in.

A kilometer toward the headland, then home: they wade out,
And plunge. All wordless, this—
In a world where all words would be
Without meaning, and all they long to hear
Is the gull's high cry
Of mercilessly joyful veracity
To fill the hollow sky.

*

Side by side, stroke by stroke, in a fading light they move.
The sea pours over each stroke's frail groove.
Blackly, the headland looms. The first star is declared.
It is white above the mountain mass.
Eyes starward fixed, they feel the sea's long swell
And the darkling drag of the nameless depth below.
They turn the headland, with starlight the only light
    they now know.

At arch-height of every stroke, at each fingertip, hangs
One drop, and the drops—one by one—are
About to fall, each a perfect universe defined
By its single, minuscule, radiant, enshrinèd star.

2. LOOKING NORTHWARD, AEGEANWARD:
NESTLINGS ON SEACLIFF

Chalky, steel-hard, or glass-slick, the cliff
That you crawl up, inch up, or clamber, till now,
Arms outspread, you cling to rotting scrub roots, and at last
See what you'd risked neck to see, the nub
Of rock-shelf outthrust from the shaded recess where,
From huddle of trash, dried droppings, and eggshell, lifts
The unfeathered pitiless weakness of necks that scarcely uphold
The pink corolla of beak-gape, the blind yearning lifeward.

In sun-blast, around and above, weave
The outraged screams that would net your head,
And wings slash the air with gleaming mercilessness,
While for toehold, or handhold, downward you grope,
Or for purchase to pause on and turn to the sun-crinkled sea,
To watch it fade northward into the
Horizon's blue ambiguity. You think
How long ago galleys—slim, black, bronze-flashing—bore
Northward too, and toward that quarter's blue dazzle of distance.
Or of a tale told.

And then think how, lost in the dimness of aeons, sea sloshed
Like suds in a washing machine, land heaved, and sky
At noon darkened, and darkness, not like any metaphor, fell,
And in that black fog gulls screamed as the feathers of gull-wing
From white flash to flame burst. That was the hour
When rooftree or keystone of palaces fell, and

Priest's grip drew backward curls of the king's son until
Throat-softness was tightened, and the last cry
Was lost in the gargle of blood on bronze blade. The king,
In the mantle, had buried his face. But even
That last sacrifice availed naught. Ashes
Would bury all. Cities beneath sea sank.

In some stony, high field, somewhere, eyes,
Unbelieving, opened. They saw, first,
The sky. Stared long. How little
They understood. But, slowly, began,
In new ignorance, the agony of Time.

You think of the necks, unfeathered and feeble, upholding
The pink corolla of beak-gape—that blind yearning lifeward.

II

PARADOX OF TIME

BLESSÈD ACCIDENT

Even if you are relatively young—say,
Nel mezzo del camin—and are not merely as

Blank of curiosity, and soul, as
A computer, you have, in fleeting moments of icy

Detachment, looking backward on
The jigsaw puzzle, wondered how you got where you now are,

And have tried to distinguish between logic
And accident. Are you, after storm, some fragment

Of wreckage stranded on a lost beach, though now perhaps in
The new, benign, but irrelevant, sunlight, in croon and whisper

Too late lulled, as wavelets gently, apologetically,
Approach and retreat on the sand?

Or, pack on back, bare knees scraped and bruised,
One hand somewhat bloody, are you now standing

On the savage crag to survey, at last,
The forest below, where the trail dies, and farther,

Lower, beyond that, the blue and glittering sinuosity
Of the river, where only yesterday you bathed? And beyond,

*

Fields brown where the plow had been set, houses
Shrinking to pin-point white dots in distance,

The slow bulge of earth purged blue
To join the heavenly blue, no certain

Horizon to be defined? Or what is the
Image that coagulates in your mind

As relevance? But one thing is sure, success,
Particularly of a vulgar order, tends

To breed complacency in the logic of
Your conduct of life. Congratulations! But,

In deepest predawn dark, have you
Grasped out and found the hand, clasped it, and lain

Hearing no sound but breath's rhythm near, and,
Gazing toward a ceiling you cannot see but know is there, felt

Slow tears swell, like bursting buds of April, in
Your eyes, your heart, and felt breath stop before

That possibility, doomful, of joy, and the awful illogic of
The tremor, the tremble, of God's palsied hand shaking

The dice-cup? Ah, blessèd accident!

PARADOX OF TIME

I. GRAVITY OF STONE AND ECSTASY OF WIND

Each day now more precious will dawn,
And loved faces turn dearer still,
And when sunlight is withdrawn,
There, over the mountain's black profile,

The western star reigns
In splendor, benign, arrogant,
And the fact that it disdains
You, and your tenement

Of flesh, should instruct you in
The paradox of Time,
And the doubleness wherein
The fleshly glory may gleam.

Sit on the floor with a child.
Hear laugh that creature so young.
See loom its life-arch, and wild
With rage, speak wild words sprung

From vision, and thus atone
For all folly now left behind.
Learn the gravity of stone.
Learn the ecstasy of wind.

Learn the law of attrition,
Learn that the mountain's crag-jut,
In that altitude of pride,
Knows the sledge and gnaw of seasons,
Each in its enmity.
Do you know how a particle,
How rain-washed downward, and down,
Is seized by the stream that boils
And roils in tumultuous white
Of flung spray, down the chasm
To reach falls that, airward, leap,
Then plunge, in incessant thunder,
To the swirl of blind mist below?
Do you know how in the heart
Of the river's majestic, slow
Flow riding, it does not know
Desire or destination?
In the broad estuary
Which, rapt and somnambulistic
Under the glitter of sun,
Moves musing seaward, it
Is borne: to enter unto
The dark inwardness of sea-wisdom
Far from the breakers' roar
And anger hurled against
Whatsoever headland or rock-shore,

And below, below, how far
From the surface agitation
Perceived by sun or star,
It moves in sea-wisdom's will.
Or hangs still, if that is the will.

As aeons pass, in a time
Unpredictable, it may be,
In turn and churn of the globe,
A single, self-possessed grain
Of sand on an unmapped strand,
White but backed by shadow
And depth of rain-jungle, and
The utterance of the victim
When, in nocturnal prowl-time,
It feels the fang at the throat.

Day dawns, and then the sand-grain
Exposes the glaze of a tiny
And time-polished facet that now
Will return from its minimal mirror
The joy of one ray from above,
But no more joy for this than
When tropic constellations,
Wheeling in brilliant darkness,
Strike one ray at that same facet
That, across howling light-years,
Makes what answer it can—
With the same indifferent joy.

For safe, safe in this asylum
Of self that is non-self, it lies
On a beach where no foot may come.

At the time of sinew dry
And crank, you may try
To think of a snow-peak glimpsed
Through a sudden aperture
In clouds, and one last sun-shaft
Flung to incarnadine
In glory that far, white
Arrogance before
Clouds close.
         Or try,
As you stare at an evening sky,
To put your mind on those
Who once stood
Erect and prophetic in
Age's long irony.
Try to name their names, or **try**
To think of the nameless ones
You never knew.
           I knew
One once, old, old, alone
In his unselfed, iron will,
Who once had said: "To deny
The self is all." So
He sat alone in that spot
Of refuge for life's discards,
His only joy a book or

Thought of the living and dead
He loved. No—one companion
He had, closer than hands,
Or feet: the cancer of which
Only he knew.
It was his precious secret.

It was as though he leaned
At a large mysterious bud
To watch, hour by hour,
How at last it would divulge
A beauty so long withheld—
As I once had sat
In a room lighted only by
Two candlesticks, and
Two flames, motionless, rose
In the summer night's breathlessness.
Three friends and I, we sat
With no conversation, watching
The bud of a century plant
That was straining against the weight
Of years, slow, slow, in silence,
To offer its inwardness.
The whiskey burned in our throats.

So the man I knew, in daily
Courtesy, lived until
The day, when, at his desk
In his cramped sitting room, he
Collapsed and, unconscious, slid
To the floor, pen yet in hand.
They revived him only for
The agony of the end.

At last, the injection.
*

I saw the end. Later,
I found the letter, the first
Paragraph unfinished. I saw
The ink-slash from that point
Where the unconscious hand had dragged
The pen as he fell. I saw
The salutation. It was:
"Dear Son."
           The shimmering
White petal—the golden stamen—
Were at last, in triumph,
Divulged. On the dusty carpet.

SMALL ETERNITY

The time comes when you count the names—whether
Dim or flaming in the head's dark, or whether
In stone cut, time-crumbling or moss-glutted.
You count the names to reconstruct yourself.

But a face remembered may blur, even as you stare
At a headstone. Or sometimes a face, as though from air,
Will stare at you with a boyish smile—but, not
Stone-moored, blows away like dandelion fuzz.

It is very disturbing. It is as though you were
The idiot boy who ventures out on pond-ice
Too thin, and hears here—hears there—the creak
And crackling spread. That is the sound Reality

Makes as it gives beneath your metaphysical
Poundage. Memory dies. Or lies. Time
Is a wind that never shifts airt. Pray only
That, in the midst of selfishness, some

Small act of careless kindness, half-unconscious, some
Unwitting smile or brush of lips, may glow
In some other mind's dark that's lost your name, but stumbles
Upon that momentary Eternity.

BASIC SYLLOGISM

Down through the latticework of leaves,
Dark in shade, golden in sunlight,
Through an eyelid half sleeping, the eye receives
News that the afternoon blazes bright.

It blazes in traumatic splendor—
A world ablaze but not consumed,
As though combustion had no end, or
Beginning, and from its ash resumed

The crackling rush of youthful flare.
Far off, a river, serpentine
In flame, threads fields of grass-green glare,
And farther, mountain cliffs incline

To catch the lethal intimation
Of sunset's utterance for climax.
I lie, and think how soon the sun
Its basic syllogism enacts.

I lie, and think how flesh and bone,
And even the soul, in its own turn,
Like faggots bound, on what hearthstone,
In their combustion, flameless, burn.

SITTING ON FARM LAWN ON
SUNDAY AFTERNOON

The old, the young—they sit.
And the baby on its blanket

Blows a crystalline
Bubble to float, then burst

Into air's nothingness.
Under the maples they sit,

As the limpid year uncoils
With a motion like motionlessness,

While only a few maple leaves
Are crisping toward yellow

And not too much rust yet
Streaks the far blades of corn.

The big white bulldog dozes
In a patch of private shade.

The afternoon muses onward,
Past work, past week, past season,

Past all the years gone by,
And delicate feminine fingers,

*

Deft and ivory-white,
And fingers steely, or knobbed

In the gnarl of arthritis, conspire
To untangle the snarl of years

Which are their past, and the past
Of kin who in dark now hide,

Yet sometimes seem to stare forth
With critical, loving gaze,

Or deeper in darkness weep
At wisdom they learned too late.

Is all wisdom learned too late?
The baby lalls to itself,

For it does not yet know all
The tales and contortions of Time.

Nor do I, who sit here alone,
In another place, and hour.

III

EVENTS

GOING WEST

Westward the Great Plains are lifting, as you
Can tell from the slight additional pressure
The accelerator requires. The sun,
Man to man, stares you straight in the eye, and the
Ribbon of road, white, into the sun's eye
Unspools. Wheat stubble behind,
Now nothing but range land. But,
With tire song lulling like love, gaze riding white ribbon, forward
You plunge. Blur of burnt goldness
Past eye-edge on each
Side back-whirling, you arrow
Into the heart of hypnosis.

This is one way to write the history of America.

It was that way that day—oh, long
Ago. I had to slap
The back of my neck to stay awake,
Eyes westward in challenge to sun-gaze, lids
Slitted for sight. The land,
Beyond miles of distance, fled
Backward to whatever had been,
As though Space were Time.

Now do I see the first blue shadow of foothills?
Or is that a cloud line?
When will snow, like a vision, lift?

*

I do not see, sudden out of
A scrub clump, the wing-burst. See only
The bloody explosion, right in my face,
On the windshield, the sun and
The whole land forward, forever,
All washed in blood, in feathers, in gut-scrawl.

It is, of course, a fool pheasant.

Hands clamping the wheel with a death grip
To hold straight while brakes scream, I,
With no breath, at the blood stare. The ditch
Is shallow enough when the car, in the end, rolls in.

Clumps of old grass, old newspaper, dry dirt—
All this got the worst off. Slowly,
Red sunset now reddening to blood streaks,
Westward the car moved on. Blood
Fried on the glass yet stove-hot. For the day—
It had been a scorcher. Later,
Handfuls of dry dirt would scrape off the fried blood.
Eventually, water at a gas station.

Even now, long afterward, the dream.

I have seen blood explode, blotting out sun, blotting
Out land, white ribbon of road, the imagined
Vision of snowcaps.

NAMELESS THING

I have no name for the nameless thing
That after midnight walks the house, usually
Soundless, but sometimes a creak on tiptoed stair,
Or sometimes like breath screwed down to a minimum.

But sometimes in silence the effluvium
Of its being is enough, perhaps with a pale,
Not quite sickening sweetness as though left
By funeral flowers, or sometimes like sweat

Under gross armpits. It is the odor of
A real existence lost in the unreality
Of dead objects of day that now painfully try to stir
In darkness. Every stone has its life, we know.

Barefoot, in darkness, I walk the house, a heavy
Poker seized from the hearth. I stand
Just by the door that seems ready to open.
I wait for the first minute motion, first whisper of hinges.

I hold my breath. I am ready. I think of blood.
I fling the door open. Only a square
Of moonlight lies on the floor inside. All is in order.
I go back to bed. I hear the blessèd heart beat there.
*

But once, on a very dark night, it was almost different.
That night I was certain. Trapped in a bathroom!
I snatched the door open, weapon up, and yes, by God!—
But there I stood staring into a mirror. Recognition

Came almost too late. But how could I
Have been expected to recognize what I am?
In any case, that was what happened. I now lie
Rigid abed and hear namelessness stalk the dark house.

I wonder why it cannot rest.

RUMOR VERIFIED

Since the rumor has been verified, you can, at least,
Disappear. You will no longer be seen at the Opera,
With your head bowed studiously, to one side a little,
Nor at your unadvertised and very exclusive
Restaurant, discussing wine with the sommelier,
Nor at your club, setting modestly forth your subtle opinion.

Since the rumor has been verified, you can try, as in dream,
To have lived another life—not with the father
Of rigid self-discipline, and x-ray glance,
Not with the mother, overindulgent and pretty,
Who toyed with your golden locks, slipped money on the side,
And waved a witch's wand for success, and a rich marriage.

Since the rumor has been verified, you may secretly sneak
Into El Salvador, or some such anguished spot,
Of which you speak the language, dreaming, trying to believe
That, orphaned, you grew up in poverty and vision, struggling
For learning, for mankind's sake. Here you pray with the sick,
    kiss lepers.

Since the rumor has been verified, you yearn to hold
A cup of cold water for the dying man to sip.
You yearn to look deep into his eyes and learn wisdom.
Or perhaps you have a practical streak and seek

Strange and derelict friends, and for justification lead
A ragtag squad to ambush the uniformed patrol.

Well, assuming the rumor verified—that may be
The only logical course: at any price,
Even bloodshed, however ruthless, to change any dominant order
And the secret corruption of power that makes us what we seem.
Yes, what is such verification against a strength of will?

But even in face of the rumor, you sometimes shudder,
Seeing men as old as you who survive the terror
Of knowledge. You watch them slyly. What is their trick?
Do they wear a Halloween face? But what can you do?
Perhaps pray to God for strength to face the verification
That you are simply a man, with a man's dead reckoning,
        nothing more.

SUNSET SCRUPULOUSLY OBSERVED

A flycatcher, small, species not identified, is perched,
Unmoving but for tiny turn and scanning
Twist of head, on the topmost twig, dead,
Of the tall, scant-leafed, and dying poplar. It
Is a black point against the cloud-curdled drama
Of sunset over dark heave
Of the mountain.

The brook, in melodious meditation, unseen,
Moves in its little gorge now brimming
With shadow. The meditation will
Continue nightlong.

The sun itself now gone, rays angle upward
From beyond the mountain. They probe,
Authoritatively, the high clouds.

A jet, military no doubt, appears high, eastward.
It creeps across the sky, ten minutes by my watch,
Uncoiling a white trail, unmoved in unmoving air.
Against paling, skim-milk blue of high sky
That is above cloud-curdle, the jet moves. The trail
Is like a decisive chalk mark that disappears
In penetrating a drift of cloud that is
Heavy, black-bellied, black on edge
Eastward, but westward with

Ragged margin inflamed by the flush of
One high-angled ray. The flush fades slowly
To gold as the jet and white trail emerge
Into that ray, and the previously
Invisible fuselage bursts
On vision, like polished silver. It proceeds
Into the dark cloud now crouching on the horizon, waiting—
Just north of the last struggle of glory.

Nearer, much nearer, five swifts, blunt-bodied like
Five tiny attack planes, zip by in formation,
Wings back-curved and pointed, twitching
In short, neurotic strokes at high speed. Their twitter
Is a needle-sharp, metallic sound.

The first bird, once silhouetted on the dying poplar's top twig,
Is gone. He is gone to fulfill his unseeable and lethal
Obligation, alone.

The evening slowly, soundlessly, closes. Like
An eyelid.

MINNEAPOLIS STORY

To John Knox Jessup

Whatever pops into your head, and whitely
Breaks surface on the dark stream that is you,

May do to make a poem—for every accident
Yearns to be more than itself, yearns,

In the way you dumbly do, to participate
In the world's blind, groping rage toward meaning, and once,

Long years ago, in Minneapolis,
Dark falling, snow falling to celebrate

The manger-birth of a babe in that snowless latitude,
Church bells vying with whack of snow-chains on

Fenders, there I, down a side street,
Head thrust into snow-swirl, strove toward Hennepin.

There lights and happiness most probably were—
But I was not thinking of happiness, only of

High-quality high-proof and the gabble in which
You try to forget that something inside you dies.

Then—hell!—it's one knee down, half-sprawled,
    one hand on a hump,
The hump human. Unconscious, but,

*

With snow scraped off, breath yet, and the putrid stink of
Non-high-quality, and vomit. So run, stumbling,

Toward Hennepin, shouting, "Police!"
"Oh, Christ," the ambulance driver says, "another one!"

"Gonna live?" I ask. "Not if he's lucky," the paramedic
Says. Slams door. Tires skid. That's all.

So half a continent, and years, away, and a different
Season too, I sit and watch

The first gold maple leaf descend athwart
My evergreens, and ponder

The mystery of Time and happiness and death.
My friend is just dead. And I wonder why

That old white bubble now arises, bursts
On my dark and secret stream. And why, again waiting alone, I see

The nameless, outraged, upturned face, where, blessèd
In shadow, domed architecture of snow, with scrupulous care,

Is minutely erected on each closed eye.
I had wiped them clear, just a moment before.

MOUNTAIN MYSTERY

On the mountain trail, all afternoon,
Gravel, uncertain, grinds under hoof.
On left side, with scrub growth, the cliff hangs.
On right, hypnotic emptiness.

Far down, in distance, a stream uncoils,
Like nothing more than a glittering wire
Tangled in stone-slots, lost on the plain,
In distance dissolved, or down canyon, gone.

You stop. You turn and know what already
You know: snow commanding west ranges, sun
Yet high. Again, eastward turn, and the sun's
Hot hand, fingers spread, is pressed against your shoulders.

Soaring in sunlight, eastward, the eagle
Swings to a height invisible
Except when light catches a bright flash of wing.
You open your lips in infinite thirst for

The altitude's wine. All, all of the past
Is gone. Yet what is the past but delusion?
Or future? In timeless light the world swims.
Alone, alone, you move through the timeless
*

Light. Toward what? The ranch in the valley,
Some ten miles away—what but delusion?
Alone, but not alone, for if
You lift your eyes, you see, some forty

Feet off, her there—unless, of course,
The track now rounds an abutment, and she
Has ceased to exist, and you are alone
In the world's metaphysical beauty of light.

Only alone do you then think of love.
Eyes shut, you think how, in saddle that narrow
Waist sways. You think how, when soon the trail straightens,
She will lean back to smile. Her eyes will be bright.

You pass the abutment. Beyond, the great mesa
Sinks blue. The world falls away, falls forever.
But she sways in the saddle, turns, smiles, and your heart
Leaps up. Then cries out: *Oh, what is enough?*

That night you will lie in your bed, not alone—
But alone. In dark paradox, you lie
And think of the screaming gleam of the world
In which you have passed alone, lost—

And in dark, lost, lain, hearing frailty of breath beside.

CONVERGENCES

By saplings I jerked and swung
Or by vine-twists and rock-snags clung,

Letting myself swing and slide
Down the mountain's near-vertical side

To the *V*-deep gorge below,
Where I caught water's glint and flow,

While last spit on the tongue dried,
And the empty canteen at my side

Clinked dry as Hell at high noon
When rain's not predicted soon,

And the literal sun that hung
At zenith guaranteed the lung

Only air like a blast-furnace blast.
Well, I got down there at last.

Belly-down, I drowned my face
Beneath that clear element's grace

And let arms relax and go
To waver like weeds in the flow,

*

Till I had to come up for air.
Across the riffle and glint there

Just as I came to raise
My mouth for sweet breath, that gaze,

Wolfish and slit-eyed, fixed on me.
My blood stiffened up like jelly.

There across lips, gray and dry,
A gray tongue-tip warily

Slid back and forth. Slow to heal,
Yellow as piss or orange peel,

From eye-edge to mouth-edge, the slash in
Flesh defined a man born not to win,

But he plunged across the stream—
In that instant less real than a dream

Till he said: "What you got in that sack?"
I'm yet down, he kicked my knapsack.

"Git it off and give it here quick!
You damned little Boy Scout prick—

"Or whatever you are." "But I'm not,"
I yelled, "any durn Boy Scout!"

"Well, prick," he said, and the knife,
At his touch, sprang to sun-flaming life.

My sandwich he ate, but spat
Out the milk. Said: "Christ!" And with that
*

Had busted my thermos, on stone.
Again spat. Then rose. Was gone.

He splashed back across the stream.
Yes—all had seemed a dream.

I didn't get up, just lay
Staring up at the heart-height of day,

Thinking: "Had me a .38,
And I'd plugged him while he ate."

A buzzard, high, cruised the sky,
I heard a far joree cry.

Then I plunged across as he'd done,
Clambered brush to the ballast-stone

Of the hidden railroad track.
Now I saw him a half-mile back,

A dot in the distance of sun
Where two gleaming rails became one

To impale him in the black throat
Of a tunnel that sucked all to naught.

I turned my own way to go
Down a track that I did not yet know

Was the track I was doomed to go
In my biologic flow—

Down the tunnel of year, day, hour,
Where the arch sags lower and lower,
*

Sometimes darker by day than by night,
Where right may be wrong or wrong right,

Where the wick sparely feeds the flame,
And Hope does not know its own name,

Where sometimes you find that at length
You're betrayed less by weakness than strength,

And though silence, like wax, fills the ear,
Sometimes you think you can hear

The mathematical drip
Of moisture, or shale above slip,

Or rock grind. And your heart gives a cry
For height, for some snow-peak high,

And lighted by one great star.
Then in dark you ask who you are.

You ask that, but yet undefined,
See, in the dark of your mind,

As you once saw, long years back,
The converging gleams of the track

That speared that small dot yonder
So that it was sucked under

The mountain—into that black hollow
Which led where you cannot know.

IV

A POINT NORTH

VERMONT THAW

A soft wind southwesterly, something like
The wind in the Far West they call the *chinook,*
About three o'clock, we yet high on the mountain,
Began. Snow softened to burden our snowshoes.

If then you stood perfectly still, so still
You could hear your own heart, each stroke by stroke,
You could hear the forest of spruces—*drip,*
Drip, drip—and you felt that all you had lived was

That sound hung in motionless silence. You held
Your breath to be sure you could hear your own heart
Maintain, with no falter, the rhythm that drops
Now defined. Were you sure you remembered your name?

But there was the *A*-frame, the camp, snow sliding
Down the steep roof-pitch with channels of black
Where all winter your eye had loved whiteness, and now
Roof-edges dripped in a rhythm that redefined

Life as blankness. In dingy pink pillows of mist,
Sun sank, and you felt it gasping for breath.
You felt it might suffocate, not rise
Again. Inside the *A*-frame you found
*

Yourself sweating, though only one eye of a coal
Yet winked. You built it up only enough
To cook by, racked up the snowshoes—all this
With no word. What word is to say when the world

Has lost heart, is dripping, is flowing, is counting
Its pulse away? Cooking is but
An irritation. The predinner whiskey
Is tongue-hot but tangless, like rotgut—not what

It is. When you turn on the hi-fi, your friend
Says: "None of that ordure tonight." In silence
You eat—silence except for the eaves-drip.
No need to bank fire on a night like this.

You wake in the dark to the rhythm of eaves.
Can you comfort yourself by thinking of spring?
Of summer's fecundity and body's plunge
Into silvery splash-spray? Of gold and flame

In benediction of autumn? Of snow's first
Night-whisper, dawn reddening peak-thrust? No—eaves,
To your heart, say now only one thing. Say: *drip*.
You must try to think of some other answer, by dawn.

CYCLE

Perhaps I have had enough of summer's
Swelling complacency, and the endless complex
And self-indulgent daubs and washes of the palette of green.
If only one birch, maple, or high poplar leaf would stir

Even in its sun-glittering green!—but this air
Is paralyzed, and the fat porcupine stops, does not even waddle
Across the lost clearing, where only a chimney now crumbles,
To the log backhouse that by his tooth, long back, is well scored.

He, in characteristic passionlessness, now stands, and
Spine-tips gleam white in sunlight. He waits,
In self-sufficient, armed idleness, memento
Of another age. Birds, in virid heat of shade,

At this hour, motionless, gasp. The beak
Droops open, silent. The sun
Is pasted to the sky, cut crude as a child's collage.
Birds have no instruction in

Cycles of nature, or astronomy. They do not know
That a time for song will, again, come, or time to zigzag
After insects at sunset. They know only the gasping present,
Like an empire unwittingly headed for the dump-heap

*

Of history. Green hides rock-slide, cliff, ledge. On the mountain,
On one ledge visible, with glasses I see propped, leaning
Back like a fat banker in his club window,
A bear, scratching his belly, in infinite ease, sun or not.

I hear the faint ripple of water
By stones, of which the tops are hot as stove-lids.
I want to lie in water, black, deep, under a bank of shade,
Like a trout. I want to breathe through gills.

But I know that snow, like history, will come. I know that ice-crust
On it will creak and crackle to snowshoes, and that
Breath will be white in air, under sky bluer than
God's Nordic eye. My hearth-wood will be stacked in an
        admirable row.

In the dark I will wake, on the hearth see last coals glow.

SUMMER RAIN IN MOUNTAINS

A dark curtain of rain sweeps slowly over the sunlit mountain.
It moves with steady dignity, like the curtain over the
Great window of a stately drawing room, or across a proscenium.

The edge of the drawn curtain of rain is decisive
Like a knife-edge. Soon it will slice the reddening sun across
      with delicate
Precision. On the yet sunlit half of the mountain miles of
      massed trees,

Glittering in green as they forever climb toward gray ledges,
Renounce their ambition, they shudder and twist, and
The undersides of leaves are grayly exposed to crave mercy.

The sun disappears. Chairs are withdrawn from the sun-deck.
A whisper is moving through the wide air. The whole event
Is reminding you of something. Your breathing becomes
      irregular, and

Your pulse flutters. Conversation dies. In silence, you peccantly
Spy on faces that were once familiar. They seem
To huddle together. One has a false face. What,

In God's name, are you trying to remember? Is it
Grief, loss of love long back, loss of confidence in your mission? Or
A guilt you can't face? Or a nameless apprehension

*

That, doglike, at night, in darkness, may lie at the foot of your bed,
Its tail now and then thumping the floor, with a sound that
Wakes you up? Your palms may then sweat. The wild

Thought seizes you that this may be a code. It may be a secret
    warning.
A friend is addressing you now. You miss the words. You
Apologize, smile. The rain hammers the roof,

Quite normally. The little group is quite normal too, some
With highballs in hand. One laughs. He is a philosopher.
You know that fact because a philosopher can laugh at

Anything. Suddenly, rain stops. The sun
Emerges like God's calm blessedness that spills
On the refurbished glitter of mountain. Chairs

Are taken again out to the sun-deck.
Conversation becomes unusually animated as all await the glory
Of sunset. You pull yourself together. A drink helps.

After all, it's the sort of thing that may happen to anybody.
And does.

VERMONT BALLAD:
CHANGE OF SEASON

All day the fitful rain
Had wrought new traceries,
New quirks, new love-knots, down the pane.

And what do I see beyond
That fluctuating gray
But a world that seems to be God-abandoned—

Last leaf, rain-soaked, from my high
Birch falling, the spruce wrapped in thought,
And the mountain dissolving rain-gray to gray sky.

In the gorge, like a maniac
In sleep, the stream grinds its teeth,
As I lay a new log at the fireplace back.

It is not that I am cold:
But that I think how the flux,
Three quarters now of a century old,

Has faithfully swollen and ebbed,
In life's brilliantly flashing red
Through all flesh, in vein and artery webbed.

But now it feels viscous and gray
As I watch the gray of the world,
And that thought seems soaked in my brain to stay.

*

But who is master here?
The turn of the season, or I?
What lies in the turn of the season to fear?

If I set muzzle to forehead
And pull the trigger, I'll see
The world in a last flood of vital red—

Not gray—that cataracts down.
No, I go to the windowpane
That rain's blurring tracery claims as its own,

And stare up the mountain track
Till I see in the rain-dusk, trudging
With stolid stride, his bundle on back,

A man with no name, in the gloom,
On an errand I cannot guess.
No sportsman—no! Just a man in his doom.

In this section such a man is not an uncommon sight.
In rain or snow, you pass, and he says: "Kinda rough tonight."

V

IF THIS IS
THE WAY IT IS

QUESTIONS YOU MUST
LEARN TO LIVE PAST

Have you ever clung to the cliffside while,
Past star-death at midnight and clouds, the darkness

Curdles and coils, and wind off the sea, caterwauling, swings in
To bulge your shirt belt-free, while claws

Scratch at eyeballs, and snag at loosening stone—
In Hell's own conspiracy with

The five-fathom, lethal, up-lunges of sea-foam fanged white,
That howls in its hunger for blood?

Have you stood by a bed whereon
Your father, unspeakable anguish past, at length

To the syringe succumbs, and your sister's
Nails clench in your biceps? Then, crazed, she cries:

"But it's worse—oh, it's driving pain deeper,
Deeper to hide from praying, or dying, or God—

"Oh, worse!" Or have you remembered the face
Of an old, loved friend, now drowned and glimmering under

Time's windless wash? Then cannot summon the name?
Have you dreamed that you are a child again
*

And calling in darkness, but nobody comes?
Have you ever seen your own child, that first morning, wait

For the school bus? Have you stood in your garden in autumn,
At some last chore, and in the junipers found

Where a three-foot snake—a big garter, no doubt—
Has combed its old integument off in the convenient prickles?

Would you hold that frayed translucence up,
Beautiful, meaningless, blessed in the mellow light,

And feel your heart stop? And not know why?
Or think that this bright emptiness

Is all your own life may be—or will be—when,
After the fable of summer, a lithe sinuosity

Slips down to curl in some dark, wintry hole, with no dream?

AFTER RESTLESS NIGHT

In darkness we cannot see
How, all night long, slow ages shift and crumble
Into the noble indifference of Eternity,
But all night do see how the dream, anguished or funny, strives
To decode the clutter of our lives.

So, shifting and crumbling too,
We let ourselves flow from ourselves into
The vast programming of the firmament
Or of our secret channeling of blood. But do
We even know the meaning of

A single comet's mathematical prowl?

Nor can we in the silence of night hear
How aeons are de-leafing, year by year,
To build the rotting mulch of History.
So now in the trough of Time, as of earth or water, we
Lie—no wind, no wave,
To stir us in that nocturnal grave,

And consciousness loses faith in itself.

Finally, comes first dawn-streak, sallow
Or slow glow from one small cinder of red
Beyond black trees. If you rise to allow

Nature her due, you may lift a curtain by the bed
To reassure yourself that the world indeed
Exists. Then back to bed,
Where warmth of pillow yet summons your head,
And consciousness for deeper concealment gnaws
Into the fat dark of your skull.
Traffic, far off, begins to whisper, like rumor of Truth.
It is a rumor of which the world is often full.

It is a rumor we might as well take at face value.

You shut your eyes and try
To believe in that possibility.
Meanwhile,
Great plains of grass stretch far
Away, like the pampas in Argentina. In steel-bright air
High snow shines moonlit, and a star
Is blue, not near setting. Somewhere,
Seals bark on a dawn-rock. A foot
Is set soundless to earth in a forest in Asia. Your mother
And father, though in their privileged privacy, turn not
One to the other.

They lie sunk in their cogitation.
Perhaps all they have is their future, the past being gone.
I advise no distraction to their frozen agon.
Perhaps each, in prayer for you, is locked alone.

Meanwhile the alarm clock goes off.
It has something to say.
It tells you what you are and what you will be all day.

Meanwhile shut eyes and think of a face you truly love,
Or at least think of something you must do as soon as you can move.

No use falling back. It is now impossible,
No matter how hard you try, to think of truly nothing.

WHAT WAS THE THOUGHT?

The thought creeps along the baseboard of the dark mind.
Through one failed juncture of curtains, the winter moon, full,
     strikes.
A white line, blade-sharp, streaks the floor,
But sheds no light. You do not see what creeps. What!—
Did it briefly scurry then? Or was that the wind
Momentarily gusting through bare boughs of the season? You think
Of the little heart, more delicate, more
Intricate, than a Swiss watch, beating
Somewhere down in the dark. You cannot, of course,
Hear it. So you listen to your own heart.
It is more gross in the darkness. What
Is it afraid of? It is warm
In its own bed, in its loving flesh. Flesh
Fondles the heart. The heart does not need to creep
Along a baseboard, hungry in the middle
Of the night, in a strange house. You feel
Your heart settle to the old guaranteed rhythm.
You know that constellations also are
Steady about their allotted business. Your children
Are healthy. They do well at school. Your
Wife is faithful. Resolutely,
You try not to wonder
What she thinks about. Suddenly,
You feel like weeping. But
You go to sleep.

*

Only after first dawn do you wake to the soft bounce
On the bed, and the special throaty mew
Of announcement. Yes, you know
What that means. It is triumph. You
Turn on the light. The pussycat
Crouches at your knees, proud, expecting
Praise. There, blood streaking the counterpane, it lies—
Skull crushed, partly eviscerated.

DEAD HORSE IN FIELD

In the last, far field, half-buried
In barberry bushes red-fruited, the thoroughbred
Lies dead, left foreleg shattered below knee,
A 30.06 in heart. In distance,
I now see gorged crows rise ragged in wind. The day
After death I had gone for farewell, and the eyes
Were already gone—that
The beneficent work of crows. Eyes gone,
The two-year-old could, of course, more readily see
Down the track of pure and eternal darkness.

A week later I couldn't get close. The sweet stink
Had begun. That damned wagon mudhole
Hidden by leaves as we galloped—I found it.
Spat on it. As a child would. Next day
The buzzards. How beautiful in air!—carving
The slow, concentric, downward pattern of vortex, wing-glint
On wing-glint. From the house,
Now with glasses, I see
The squabble and pushing, the waggle of wattle-red heads.

At evening I watch the buzzards, the crows,
Arise. They swing black in nature's flow and perfection,
High in sad carmine of sunset. Forgiveness
Is not indicated. It is superfluous. They are
What they are.

*

How long before I go back to see
That intricate piece of
Modern sculpture, white now
By weather and sun, intricate, now
Assuming in stasis
New beauty! Then,
A year later, I'll see
The green twine of vine, each leaf
Heart-shaped, soft as velvet, beginning
Its benediction.

It thinks it is God.

Can you think of some ground on which that may be gainsaid?

IMMANENCE

Stop! Wait! Wherever you are.
Whatever your name. It may well be

At the corner of one of the Fifties and Fifth Avenue,
Where the City of Things gleams brightest, and

Your name does not matter. If you have your credit card.
But sometimes its referent is obscure to you, and then even

The card is no help. Except, of course, for the purchase. Or
The event, in fact, may well be elsewhere, at night,

In bed, and you lost and unsure what
Bed, or breath there beside, and a crusting on

Dong. Like an orchid, now darkness
Swells, benign, benign—or inimical—

In immanence. Yes, something
Plays cat-and-mouse with you, veiled, unrevealed, though you

Sometimes relax, pretend not to notice, thinking
You'll be the cat, and catch

It unawares. Unwary. Trapped
In your stratagem. For if

*

Its face is seen, name known, it,
Then powerless, like mist, may be shifted by

Whatever slight movement of air, and in anguish
Flee, with a scream of such

Desolation that a heart as horn-scabbed as yours would be stabbed
To pity. But no. You must ponder yet the teasing enigma. But

Suppose you never succeed? Or worse,
The swollen Immanence turns out to be all? Is all? And you,

Yet yearning, torn between fear
And hope, yet ignorant, will, into

The black conduit of Nature's Repackaging System, be sucked.
But that possibility is simply too distressing

To—even—be considered.

THE CORNER OF THE EYE

The poem is just beyond the corner of the eye.
You cannot see it—not yet—but sense the faint gleam,

Or stir. It may be like a poor little shivering fieldmouse,
One tiny paw lifted from snow while, far off, the owl

Utters. Or like breakers, far off, almost as soundless as dream.
Or the rhythmic rasp of your father's last breath, harsh

As the grind of a great file the blacksmith sets to hoof.
Or the whispering slither the torn morning newspaper makes,

Blown down an empty slum street in New York, at midnight,
Past dog shit and garbage cans, while the full moon,

Phthisic and wan, above the East River, presides
Over that last fragment of history which is

Our lives. Or the foggy glint of old eyes of
The sleepless patient who no longer wonders

If he will once more see in that window the dun-
Bleached dawn that promises what. Or the street corner

Where always, for years, in passing you felt, unexplained, a pang
Of despair, like nausea, till one night, late, late on that spot
*

You were struck stock-still and again felt
How her head had thrust to your shoulder, she clinging, while you,

Mechanically patting the fur coat, heard sobs, and stared up
Where tall buildings, frailer than reed-stalks, reeled among stars.

Yes, something there at eye-edge lurks, hears ball creak in socket,
Knows, before you do, tension of muscle, change

Of blood pressure, heart-heave of sadness, foot's falter, for
It has stalked you all day, or years, breath rarely heard, fangs
        dripping.

And now, any moment, great hindquarters may hunch, ready—
Or is it merely a poem, after all?

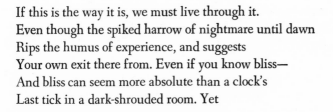

I F

If this is the way it is, we must live through it.
Even though the spiked harrow of nightmare until dawn
Rips the humus of experience, and suggests
Your own exit there from. Even if you know bliss—
And bliss can seem more absolute than a clock's
Last tick in a dark-shrouded room. Yet

If this is the way it is, let us clamber
Crag-upward from the white-slashed beach and stare
Over the tangled tumult until the soul is absorbed
Into the blue perfection of unnamable distance.
The horizon is our only dream of perfection.

If this is the way it is—and I have stood
Alone, alone, past midnight long, heart empty, in
The dark and unpopulated
Piazza Navona—and I thought: what is the use
Of remembering any dream from childhood? Particularly,
Since any particular moment would be the future all dreams
Had led to. I shut eyes now, but still see
The discarded newspaper, across the Piazza,
In a foreign language, blown
Over stones wise with suffering. The paper
Carries yesterday with it. I hear
It scrape the stones. It carries yesterday
Into tomorrow.

*

This was only a trivial incident of
My middle years. I do
Not even know why I remember it. But

If this is the way it is, we need, perhaps,
A new concept of salvation, who had long thought
Courage enough to live by. What
Can the sea tell us of a drop we cup in the hand?
What, as the tide slinks away, can a drop,
Caught on the landward side of a pebble,
Tell us of the blind depth of groan out yonder?

VI

BUT ALSO

WHAT VOICE AT MOTH-HOUR

What voice at moth-hour did I hear calling
As I stood in the orchard while the white
Petals of apple blossoms were falling,
Whiter than moth-wing in that twilight?

What voice did I hear as I stood by the stream,
Bemused in the murmurous wisdom there uttered,
While ripples at stone, in their steely gleam,
Caught last light before it was shuttered?

What voice did I hear as I wandered alone
In a premature night of cedar, beech, oak,
Each foot set soft, then still as stone
Standing to wait while the first owl spoke?

The voice that I heard once at dew-fall, I now
Can hear by a simple trick. If I close
My eyes, in that dusk I again know
The feel of damp grass between bare toes,

Can see the last zigzag, sky-skittering, high,
Of a bullbat, and even hear, far off, from
Swamp-cover, the whip-o-will, and as I
Once heard, hear the voice: *It's late! Come home.*

ANOTHER DIMENSION

Over meadows of Brittany, the lark
Flames sunward, divulging, in tinseled fragments from
That height, song. Song is lost
In the blue depth of sky, but
We know it is there at an altitude where only
God's ear may hear.

Dividing fields, long hedges, in white
Bloom powdered, gently slope to the
Blue of sea that glitters in joy of its being.

Once I lay on the grass and looked upward
To feel myself redeemed into
That world which had no meaning but itself,
As I, lying there, had only the present, no future or past.

Yes—who was the man who on the midnight street corner,
Alone, once stood, while sea-fog
Put out last lights, electric or heavenly?
Who knows that history is the other name for death?
Who, from the sweated pillow, wakes to know
How truth can lie? Who knows that jealousy,
Like a chinch-bug under the greenest turf, thrives?
Who learned that kindness can be the last cruelty?
*

I have shut my eyes and seen the lark flare upward.
All was as real as when my eyes were open.
I have felt earth breathe beneath my shoulder blades.
I have strained to hear, sun-high, that Platonic song.

It may be that some men, dying, have heard it.

GLIMPSES OF SEASONS

I. GASP-GLORY OF GOLD LIGHT

Gasp-glory of gold light of dawn on gold maple—
Now forgotten green bough-loop, fat leaf-droop, and even
The first reddening rondure of August or, slow,
The birth of the grape's yearning bulge, as summer,
Bemused in the dream of the sweetness of swelling,
Forgets to define
The mathematics of Time. But look!
At this moment you stand

On the knife-edge of no-Time.
Or is it not no-Time, but Time fulfilled?

Do not turn your head, the sun no higher will rise.
Do not listen—no heart-beat,
No watch-tick, is here to be heard.
The Self flows away into the unbruised
Guiltlessness of no-Self. Do you imagine you feel

The lips of the world bend to your own?

How long may you stand thus?—though
Such matters of vulgar logic can scarcely apply
To our category of discussion. Dismiss

The topic, and try to think, at the same moment,
Of the living and the dead.

2. SNOW OUT OF SEASON

Once in October—far too early, far out of phase—dawn
Was nothing but swirl of snow-dimness. How odd
Rose the last, lone bed of zinnias ablaze
Against God, the gray hush, and His willed dissolution!

After white earth and gray sky then came
Nothing you might call a sunset—
Just gray growing grayer to blackness.

More snow that night.

Then dawn: and sun leaped to flame,
Like the biblical strong man to run his race, but I,
Booted, in sheepskin swathed, was more modestly
Out to see the world remade
From this myth of nothingness,
Where now boughs hung heavy, white only, no crimson
Of maple, no willow by destiny yellow. The world,
White in lethalness, gleamed, except
For one thing. You know the berry
Of dogwood? Well,
Sudden on white, as on white velvet deployed,
Uncountable jewels flamed to the sun's flame.

*

Why should the heart leap? We
Are old enough to know that the world
Is only the world, and the heart
Is like fingers idly outspread while, slowly,
The gray seeds of Time, or gold grain,
Trickle through.

But we often forget.

How far a-winging to keep this appointment with April!
How much breath left in reserve to fill
The sky of washed azure and whipped-cream cumuli
With their rusty, musical, heart-plumbing cry!

On sedge, winter-bit but erect, on old cattails, they swing.
Throats throb, your field glasses say, as they cling and sing—
If singing is what you call that rusty, gut-grabbing cry
That calls on life to be lived gladly, gladly.

They twist, tumble, tangle, they glide and curvet,
And sun stabs the red splash to scarlet on each epaulet,
And the lazy distance of hills seems to take
A glint more green, and dry grass at your feet to wake.

In the vast of night, seasons later, sleet coding on pane,
Fire dead on hearth, hope banked in heart, I again
Awake, not in dream but with eyes shut, believing I hear
That rusty music far off, far off, and catch flash and fleer

Of a scarlet slash accenting the glossy black. Sleet
Continues. The heart continues its steady beat
As I burrow into the tumulus of sleep,
Where all things are buried, though no man for sure knows
    how deep.
*

The globe grinds on, proceeds with the business of Aprils and men.
Next year will redwings see me, or I them, again then?
If not, some man else may pause, awaiting that rusty, musical cry,
And catch—how gallant—the flash of epaulets scarlet against
    blue sky.

4. CROCUS DAWN

Oh, crocus dawn!—premise of promise, what
Will the day bring forth? After all the days

I have waked to in joy or pain, in anxiety or
Expectation, or with the blank check

Of a heart that flutters vacantly in
The incertitude of the future's breath,

Or blast. After the clock that pronounces
The tiny mathematical tick that is your only

Benediction in darkness, what will you wake for? After
Darkness will there come that crocus dawn

With all the shimmer and sheen of the unending promise
We wake to, to live by? Oh, crocus dawn,

May our eyes gleam once more in your light before
We know again what we must wake to be.

ENGLISH COCKER: OLD AND BLIND

With what painful deliberation he comes down the stair,
At the edge of each step one paw suspended in air,
And distrust. Does he thus stand on a final edge
Of the world? Sometimes he stands thus, and will not budge,

With a choking soft whimper, while monstrous blackness is whirled
Inside his head, and outside too, the world
Whirling in blind vertigo. But if your hand
Merely touches his head, old faith comes flooding back—and

The paw descends. His trust is infinite
In you, who are, in his eternal night,
Only a frail scent subject to the whim
Of wind, or only a hand held close to him

With a dog biscuit, or, in a sudden burst
Of temper, the force that jerks that goddamned, accurst
Little brute off your bed. But remember how you last saw
Him hesitate in his whirling dark, one paw

Suspended above the abyss at the edge of the stair,
And remember that musical whimper, and how, then aware
Of a sudden sweet heart-stab, you knew in him
The kinship of all flesh defined by a halting paradigm.

DAWN

Dawnward, I wake. In darkness, wait.
Wait for first light to seep in as sluggish and gray
As tidewater fingering timbers in a long-abandoned hulk.
In darkness I try to make out accustomed objects.

But cannot. It is as though
Their constituent atoms had gone to sleep and forgotten
Their duty of identity. But at first
Inward leakage of light they will stir

To the mathematical dance of existence. Bookcase,
Chest, chairs—they will dimly loom, yearn
Toward reality. Are you
Real when asleep? Or only when,

Feet walking, lips talking, or
Your member making its penetration, you
Enact, in a well-designed set, that ectoplasmic
Drama of laughter and tears, the climax of which always

Strikes with surprise—though the script is tattered and torn?
I think how ground mist is thinning, think
How, distantly eastward, the line of dark woods can now
Be distinguished from sky. Many
*

Distinctions will grow, and some
Will, the heart knows, be found
Painful. On the far highway,
A diesel grinds, groans on the grade.

Can the driver see color above the far woods yet?
Or will dawn come today only as gray light through
Clouds downward soaking, as from a dirty dishrag?
I think of a single tree in a wide field.

I wonder if, in this grayness, the tree will cast a shadow.
I hold up my hand. I can vaguely see it. The hand.
Far, far, a crow calls. In gray light
I see my hand against the white ceiling. I move

Fingers. I want to be real. Dear God,
To Whom, in my triviality,
I have given only trivial thought,
Will I find it worthwhile to pray that You let

The crow, at least once more, call?

MILLPOND LOST

Lucent, the millpond mirrors September blue.
Golden, the maples lean, leaf by leaf, to stare down
Through motionless air, where, in water motionless too,
Hangs the mystery of maples, golden but upside-down.

Water brims the old stone of the dam-top
Where the margin is so prettily greened by moss. But the mill,
Now long back, must have rotted away. One by one,
    old beams may drop,
Though some, mossed and leaning, through vine-ruck,
    may poke still.

They will drop, one by one, and each individual fact
Will measure out time in a place where Time seems never to die.
But wherever you are, engaged in whatever act,
You cling to the last human dream that a moment can compose
    infinity.

Try, if you can, to restore the old scene. Can you see
How the great wheel, now gone, would turn, each turn spilling
Sun-flame and silver of water, while, joyfully,
Scrawny flesh of white bodies would plunge to black water, filling

The air with maniacal shouts to shake the highest leaf?
As now you stand dreaming, one leaf, slow, releases

Its bough, and golden, luxurious, an image of joy not grief,
Scarcely in motion, descends, till even that motion on water ceases.

Shit! This scene is only imagined. Your whole life
You've not been back, and the boys, they are mostly dead,
Or good as dead, from boredom with job, children, wife,
Or booze, heart failure, cop gunfire or strikebreakers' cracked head.

In darkness, I've tried to imagine the pond after such time-lapse,
Or name the names of the boys who there shouted in joy, once.

SUMMER AFTERNOON AND HYPNOSIS

Lulled by stream-murmur and the afternoon's hypnosis
Of summer, guarded by willow shade while the sun
Westward inclines, you lie. The far world's only voice is
The muted music of sheep bells, one by one,

Threading the infinite distance of sunlight and languor.
Yes, lulled thus, your life achieves its honesty,
In which love, hate, lust, courage, cowardice, and anger,
With truth torn at last from lies, emerge from the shadowy

Mist of Time and sequence to seek in Timelessness
Each its lonely and naked reality. And your heart,
Bemused as though in a mirror's icy duress,
Seems to suspend its stroke, and your dry lips part

In a whisper of slow appalment to ask: "Was this
The life that all those years I lived, and did not know?"
Do you really think now the sun's frozen motionless?
Do you really think the stream no longer can flow?

But the heart strikes, and the world resumes its nature,
And Time swirls back like a tide more sousing than Fundy,
And whatever a man has endured he can endure,
And the shadow of that tall pine names night, and by

*

The moment it touches the mossed stone yonder, you will have
    roused
Yourself to yourself, and set foot to the mile
That leads to the roof whereunder you find enhoused
The mystery of love's redeeming smile.

VII

FEAR AND
TREMBLING

IF EVER

If ever you come where once it happened,
Pause, even briefly, and try to discover
If the heart now stalls, as once, for a lover,
It did. Or can love at the end, have an end

That is absolute? What if a mysterious
And throttling fist should now squeeze the heart,
And wrench it, and seem to tear it apart
From your bosom—what meaning for you, or for us?

Indeed, what exists in the grab-bag of pastness?
Do all things, in that vatic darkness, wear
Two faces? And frozen in hope—or despair—
Do you guess what may rise from that dark, seething vastness

That was your life? Do contradictory
Voices now at midnight utter
Doom—or promise? Or do voices merely stutter
In pronouncing the future, or history,

So that you, nightlong, in your ignorance, sweat?
What can you do? Listen!—it's true:
Seize the nettle of self, plunge then into
Cold shock of experience, like a mountain lake, and let

Stroke, after stroke, sustain you. And all else forget.

HAVE YOU EVER EATEN STARS?
(A Note on Mycology)

Scene: A glade on a bench of the mountain,
   Where beech, birch, and spruce meet
   In peace, though in peace not intermingled,
   Around the slight hollow, upholstered
   In woods-earth damp, and soft, centuries old—
   Spruce needle, beech leaf, birch leaf, ground-pine
     belly-crawling,
   And fern frond, and deadfall of birch, grass blade
   So biblically frail, and sparse in that precinct where
   The sunray makes only its brief
   And perfunctory noontide visitation.
   All, all in that cycle's beneficence
   Of being are slowly absorbed—oh, slowly—into
   What once had fed them. And now,
   In silence as absolute as death,
   Or as vision in breathlessness,
   Your foot may come. Or mine,
   As when I, sweat-soaked in summer's savagery,
   Might here come, and stand
   In that damp cool, and peace of process,
   And hear, somewhere, a summer-thinned brook
     descending,
   Past stone, and stone, its musical stair.

   But late, once in the season's lateness, I,
   After drouth had broken, rain come and gone,

And sky been washed to a blue more delicate,
Came. Stood. Stared. For now,
Earth, black as a midnight sky,
Was, like sky-darkness, studded with
Gold stars, as though
In emulation, however brief.
There, by a deer trail, by deer dung nourished,
Burst the gleam, rain-summoned,
Of bright golden chanterelles.
However briefly, however small and restricted, here was
A glade-burst of glory.

Later, I gathered stars into a basket.

Question: What can you do with stars, or glory?
I'll tell you, I'll tell you—thereof
Eat. Swallow. Absorb. Let bone
Be sustained thereof, let gristle
Toughen, flesh be more preciously
Gratified, muscle yearn in
Its strength. Let brain glow
In its own midnight of darkness,
Under its own inverted, bowl-shaped
Sky, skull-sky, let the heart
Rejoice.
        What other need now
Is possible to you but that
Of seeing life as glory?

TWICE BORN

Ah, blaze of vision in the dark hour! Once,
Some fifteen years ago, lightning, the roar
Of summer storm knifing through night forest, ricochet
Of thunder blundering among mountains, and in
Interstices of majestic racket, rain-gust on roof—and I
Was snatched from sleep. I heard
The irredeemable riot, heard
The encirclement of thunder, which, suddenly,
Was sinking to a grumble, far away. So breath
Came back, and the heart resumed normal
Function. But one last and greatest crash, as though
On our roof, as though God
Was not mocked by any easy assumption, the crash
Accompanied by a flash dazzling the dark of the room,
Objects leaping to visibility, plunging at stunned eyes,
Air smelling of electricity. This time, the end, but

Not the end. In silence, light
Was entering the room as though lightning,
Thunderless and constant, prevailed. I
Tore back the curtain, saw. A great dead pine,
Fifty yards off, a torch sky-high now. Nothing
To be done. And no need, only deciduous
Trees near, I found, and rain-drenched, safe enough.
*

Back from investigation, soaked, and hands
Chilled to the marrow, shoes squishing water, mud
Clear up to blue-jean knees, I tore
Clothes off, toweled blood-heat up, plunged
Into bed. But not to sleep, not even after
The God-ignited torch, dying, left
Only a faint flicker on the walls—and the ceiling
That I stared at with a strange shudder and excitement. But
A calm sweetness was filling the room as darkness grew
And I could not see the ceiling. Then, all
At once, I knew. I knew
The storm, and all therewith, but as
A metaphor.
        It was, I knew,
A metaphor for what, long back, I
Had undergone. I saw the fact of that.

In calmness, soon, I slept.

THE SEA HATES THE LAND

Be not deceived by the slow swell and lull of sea lolling
In moonlight off Maine, or by tropical listlessness
Of the Gulf when cesspool slick, or by muted tolling
Of fog-bell when sea scarcely breathes. Deeper process

Proceeds, as blood inwardly flows while you sleep. One thing
Remember: the sea hates the land, that arrogant, late
Intruder on solitude's deep coil, no wing
Yet between the unsleeping depth's unabat-

ing fulfillment of self and the undefinable span
Of space forever seeking self's infinite end.
You cannot blame the sea. For you, as a man,
Know that only in loneliness are you defined.

Yes, the cormorant's scream, and even the kiss at midnight,
And the hurly-burly of firmaments and men
Are froth on the surface of deepening need: so by moonlight
Swim seaward, stroke steady, breath deep, remembering when

The self had the joy of selflessness completely
Absorbed in the innocent solipsism of the sea.

AFTERWARD

After the promise has been kept, or
Broken. After the sun

Has touched the peak westward and you suddenly
Realize that Time has cut another notch

In the stick with your name on it, and you wonder
How long before you will feel the need

For prayer. After you have stumbled on the obituary
Of a once-girl, photograph unrecognizable,

Who, at night, used to come to your apartment and do
        everything but
It. Would fight like a tiger. Then weep.

Never married, but made, as the paper says,
A brilliant career, also prominent in good works. After

You have, in shame, lain awake trying to account for
Certain deeds of vanity, weakness, folly, or

Neurosis, and have shuddered in disbelief. After
You have heard the unhearable lonely wolf-howl of grief
*

In your heart, and walked a dark house, feet bare. After
You have looked down on the unimaginable expanse of polar

Icecap stretching forever in light of gray-green ambiguousness,
And, lulled by jet-hum, wondered if this

Is the only image of eternity. —Ah, menhirs, monoliths, and all
Such frozen thrusts of stone, arms in upward anguish of fantasy,
    images

By creatures, hairy and humped, on heath, on hill, in holt
Raised! Oh, see

How a nameless skull, by weather uncovered or
The dateless winds,

In the moonlit desert, smiles, having been
So long alone. After all, are you ready

To return the smile? Try. Sit down by a great cactus,
While other cacti, near and as far as distance, lift up

Their arms, thorny and black, in ritual unresting above
Tangles of black shadow on white sand, to that great orb

Of ever out-brimming, unspooling light and glow, queenly for
    good or evil, in
The forever sky. After you have sat

In company awhile, perhaps trust will grow.
Perhaps you can start a conversation of mutual comfort.

There must be so much to exchange.

VIII

CODA

FEAR AND TREMBLING

The sun now angles downward, and southward.
The summer, that is, approaches its final fulfillment.
The forest is silent, no wind-stir, bird-note, or word.
It is time to meditate on what the season has meant.

But what is the meaningful language for such meditation?
What is a word but wind through the tube of the throat?
Who defines the relation between the word *sun* and the sun?
What word has glittered on whitecap? Or lured blossom out?

Walk deeper, foot soundless, into the forest.
Stop, breath bated. Look southward, and up, where high leaves
Against sun, in vernal translucence, yet glow with the freshest
Young tint of the lost spring. Here now nothing grieves.

Can one, in fact, meditate in the heart, rapt and wordless?
Or find his own voice in the towering gust now from northward?
When boughs toss—is it in joy or pain and madness?
The gold leaf—is it whirled in anguish or ecstasy skyward?

Can the heart's meditation wake us from life's long sleep,
And instruct us how foolish and fond was our labor spent—
Us who now know that only at death of ambition does the deep
Energy crack crust, spurt forth, and leap

From grottoes, dark—and from the caverned enchainment?

ABOUT THE AUTHOR

ROBERT PENN WARREN was born in Guthrie, Kentucky, in 1905. After graduating summa cum laude from Vanderbilt University (1925), he received a master's degree from the University of California (1927), and did graduate work at Yale University (1927–28) and at Oxford as a Rhodes Scholar (B. Litt., 1930).

Mr. Warren has published many books, including ten novels, fourteen volumes of poetry, and a volume of short stories; also a play, a collection of critical essays, a biography, three historical essays, a critical book on Dreiser and a study of Melville, and two studies of race relations in America. This body of work has been published in a period of fifty-one years—a period during which Mr. Warren has also had an active career as a professor of English.

All the King's Men (1946) was awarded the Pulitzer Prize for Fiction. The Shelley Memorial Award recognized Mr. Warren's early poems. *Promises* (1957) won the Pulitzer Prize for Poetry, the Edna St. Vincent Millay Prize for the Poetry Society of America, and the National Book Award. In 1944–45 Mr. Warren was the second occupant of the Chair of Poetry at the Library of Congress. In 1952 he was elected to the American Philosophical Society; in 1959 to the American Academy of Arts and Letters; and in 1975 to the American Academy of Arts and Sciences. In 1967 he received the Bollingen Prize in Poetry for *Selected Poems: New and Old, 1923–1966,* and in 1970 the National Medal for Literature, and the Van Wyck Brooks Award for the book-length poem *Audubon: A Vision.* In 1974 he was chosen by the National Endowment for the Humanities to deliver the third Annual Jefferson Lecture in the Humanities. In 1975 he received the Emerson-Thoreau Award of the American Academy of Arts and Sciences. In 1976 he received the Copernicus Award from the Academy of American Poets, in recognition of his career but with special notice of *Or Else—Poem/Poems 1968–1974.* In 1977 he received the Harriet Monroe Prize for Poetry and the Wilma and Roswell Messing, Jr. Award. In 1979, for *Now and Then,* a book of new poems, he received his third Pulitzer Prize. In 1980 he received the Award of the Connecticut Arts Council, the Presidential Medal of Freedom, the Common Wealth Award for Literature, and the Hubbell Memorial Award (The Modern Language Association). In 1981 he was a recipient of a Prize Fellowship of the John D. and Catherine T. MacArthur Foundation.

Mr. Warren lives in Connecticut with his wife, Eleanor Clark (author of *The Bitter Box, Rome and a Villa, The Oysters of Locmariaquer, Baldur's Gate, Eyes, Etc.: A Memoir,* and *Gloria Mundi*). They have two children, Rosanna and Gabriel.